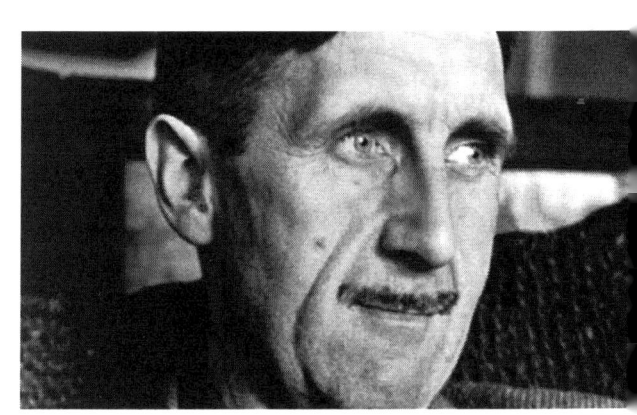

GEORGE ORWELL

***&1984*венности: A TALK BY PAUL FOOT**

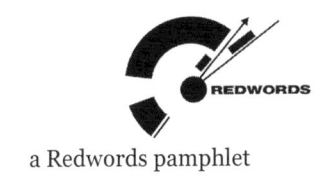

a Redwords pamphlet

George Orwell & 1984: a talk by Paul Foot
Introduction by John Rudge

a Redwords pamphlet published January 2020

ISBN: 9781912926 503
ebook: 9781912926 510
kindle: 9781912926 527

Redwords is connected to
Bookmarks: The Socialist Bookshop, 1 Bloomsbury Street,
London WC1B 3QE
https://bookmarksbookshop.co.uk

Design and production: Roger Huddle
Printed by Halstan & Co. Ltd.

Half title: George Orwell
Title: Paul Foot speaking at Students Fighting For Socialism,
University of London Union, 28th November 1998.
Photograph: Steve Eason

Acknowledgements: Many people had a hand in bringing Paul's
'lost talk' to light after so many years. Among them are Clare
Fermont, Ian Birchall, John Newsinger, Camilla Royle and Carol
Withers. My thanks to everyone involved. — John Rudge

Introduction

June 2019 marked the 70th anniversary of the publication of George Orwell's famous, dystopian novel *1984*. It is no exaggeration to say that the work causes as much argument today as it did seventy years ago. Nowhere has this controversy raged more than on the political left.

Frankly, much of the left has had an ongoing problem with Orwell and particularly with his two last, and most famous books, *Animal Farm* and *1984*. Questions have abounded – "Why did he Write Them?"; "What are They Really About?"; "Had he Renounced the Left and Joined the Cold War?"; "Is there a Political Message for Today in Them?"

It would be too easy to say that social democrats love Orwell because they believe he turned against revolution. That the Communist Parties hated Orwell's anti-Stalinism with a vengeance almost unsurpassed – their day is now gone. But Orwell and his work has also remained contested on the far left. "Was he, or was he not, one of us?" That contest has been a feature of the International Socialist (IS) tradition as much as anywhere else on the revolutionary left.

In the IS tradition's press over the years, there have been innumerable articles about or connected with George Orwell and his works. It would be fruitless to list those who see him as "one of us", those that see him as "one of them" and those that take a middle-line. Suffice it to say that there are plenty in all three camps.

One of the staunchest supporters of George Orwell within our tradition has been Paul Foot. He wrote a number of articles on Orwell both within the Party's own press and outside it. Always he was prepared to look beyond a shallow-reading of Orwell and his work. Always he was committed to seeing Orwell and his work in its proper historical context. Always he was willing to acknowledge Orwell's weaknesses as well as his strengths. I feel sure that he would have agreed with John Newsinger's description:

"Orwell, it is important to remember, was always a "work in progress". His ideas and attitudes were always developing, changing: through discussion and argument, influenced by his extensive reading and by the unfolding of events as he viewed them and participated in them." (Newsinger, 2018).

Importantly, Paul was always prepared to confront Orwell's two most difficult books, *Animal Farm*, and especially, *1984*, head-on. At no time was this more apparent than in the year 1984, when debate about the book and its meaning reached fever-pitch.

In that year Paul spoke at a number of meetings on the subject of Orwell's book. Not the least of these was a talk he gave at the SWP Rally in Skegness on Sunday 22nd April 1984. A tape and transcript of the meeting was made but, unlike other of Paul's Skegness talks, this one was never published as a Party pamphlet. The reason was euphemistically described as "....due to controversy". That controversy being, of course, the contested nature of George Orwell and of *1984* within the organisation.

I have copied the transcript of that Skegness meeting from the Bookmarks Publications archive at Warwick Modern Records Centre. It has been edited to better suit the print medium, rather than the original spoken word, but certainly without changing any of Paul's meanings. It is a delight to present it here, for Paul was surely the greatest public-speaker that the IS tradition has produced. He could electrify an audience with his words, his message, his passion and his delivery. His ability to convey an important political point in an interesting manner was second to none. How is this for a comment on democratic centralism and the SWP:

"We have a collective. I think sometimes people think that the collective is just a lot of people speaking with one voice. Now, it is a lot of people speaking with one voice, but it is very important that the one voice is divided into hundreds, if not thousands of different accents and different languages. I think people sometimes think that being in a collective enables them to surrender their duty to think each subject through. And I think the great advantage of Orwell is that he thought everything through for himself."

Above all Paul believed in what he says in this talk about communication:

"[it] should be like a window-pane. You should

be able to see through language, to its meaning. If you cannot see through language to its meaning, it is absolutely appalling."

Does the "Orwell Debate" matter? I say, unequivocally "Yes". The rise of the Far Right and Trump, the way that we are spied upon via cameras in every corner of our towns and cities, how vast amounts of data are collected about every aspect of our lives and when capitalism is destroying the very planet we live on; these are all reasons why Orwell is as relevant today as he was back in 1949. It makes the debate as important now as it ever was. And there is one person from within the IS tradition who knew exactly where he stood in that debate – Paul Foot.

John Rudge Spring 2019

Literature Cited
Newsinger, John. 2018. *Hope Lies in the Proles: George Orwell and the Left*. Pluto Press, London.

Setting the Scene

I have some news from Penguin Books which is that 1984 has been a tremendous year for the Orwell industry. I hear that from 1st September last year to 1st March this year the Penguin edition of *1984* has sold 770,000 copies. That is about four thousand copies every day being sold in this country. Since Penguin started publishing Orwell, in the 1950's, fourteen million copies of Orwell's books have been sold to people in this country – obviously that does not include what has been sold in America, where the figure is almost astronomical.

The fact is that these books, particularly *Animal Farm* and *1984*, have entered deep into the consciousness of people. There are lots of people who have perhaps only read one or two books over a period of years, and they are Orwell's *1984* or *Animal Farm*. They are really huge selling books which are very much a part of the mass culture of the country.

The SWP has built up quite a close relationship with Orwell in spite of that. You might imagine that anything that was quite such a part of mass culture would be ignored a little by us, but that is not the case. Way back in 1969, I remember Peter Sedgwick writing in *International Socialism* the first of what was to be two articles, but unfortunately the second never appeared, which was entitled "George Orwell: International Socialist?" [1].

That meant something more than what you might think it means. What it meant was: "George Orwell: Socialist Workers Party member". That is what it meant, and Peter argued, very powerfully I think, that George Orwell *does* fit into the tradition of our politics, and does come out of our same attitude to politics. You have probably read, in a recent issue of *Socialist Review*, a very good article by John Deason[2] saying roughly the same thing – and in the coming edition of *International Socialism* journal you will read a very learned article by Paul O'Flinn[3], arguing that a whole lot of what Orwell had to say, particularly about Spain, fits closely into our tradition.

I want to do something a little bit different. I do not just want to see whether Orwell was "one of us", although that will be part of it. What I also want to do is to see what it is that he has got to contribute to us, and what is it that we have got to contribute to him.

Early Days

Orwell was born in Bengal. His father worked in the Opium Department of the India Office. I will repeat that, because sometimes people do not really believe it: he worked in the *Opium* Department of the India Office – rather similar to someone saying he worked in the Heroin Department of the Department of Health and Social Security.

It is very important to understand about British imperialism in India, that the *centre* of it, at the beginning, was the destruction of the agriculture of Bengal in order that the soil could be made proper for the preparation of opium to sell to the Chinese. That was, as it were, the centrepiece of white Christian civilisation in that part of the world. If you wanted to get on in the India Office, in the India Department or the Indian government, it was quite a feather in your cap to say "Well, I'm in the Opium Department" – a very important person indeed. Symbolic, really, of what British imperialism meant in the Indian subcontinent, and Orwell was very quickly to come to grips with that.

He went to a terrible private prep school, which he described very rigorously, and then of course he went to Eton. He describes a situation in Eton and the end of his time there, when there were sixteen boys in the class and they were asked to name the ten most important people living at that time. Fifteen out of sixteen named Lenin. Now that, you might have thought, would have a profound effect upon what those boys might have done when they left Eton, but the situation then, whether or not you thought Lenin was important, was the same as it is now for people who go to Eton. Their jobs are safe. Their life is safe. If they are clever they go to university. If they are not so clever they go to university. If they are backward* they go into the army and if they are gormless they go into the Church.

Orwell was not so clever at that time. He was, I think, 138th out of 151, so he went into the army – or its equivalent, the Burmese Police, where he had those connections with the Indian subcontinent. Very quickly he came face-to-face with the reality of what British imperialism was about in Burma. He was there for four years, between 1922 and 1927, and in that time – this is an astonishing figure – there were 612 hangings of Burmese people who protested in one way or another about British imperialism. Six hundred and twelve – that is about three a week over a period of four years.

Orwell, in his capacity as police officer, saw rather a lot of this, and was shocked by it all his life. Indeed, one of the things he has got to contribute to us is consistent detestation of British imperialism, which goes right the way through his life, right the way through all his ups and downs, optimisms and pessimisms.

He wrote a book called *Burmese Days*:
"Even those bloody fools at the Club might be better company if we weren't all of us living a lie the whole time... the lie that we're here to uplift our poor black brothers instead of to rob them."

---

*Paul Foot's use of the term 'backward' in this passage is not language that we would use today, given its negative connotations for people with disabilities.

He hated it. He hated the British in Burma. He hated his fellow policemen most of all. And as soon as he got home on leave he resigned from the police force. For many years he was plunged into a sort of guilt, which you see coming out all the time in his writing, about what had happened in Burma. It made him into what he thought was a socialist. He said he was a socialist. He said that he didn't like the society, and he had heard in the way that you do if you go to public school, about the working classes. You see, the ruling class always refers to the working class as the *working classes* – there are lots of them, all jumbled up and all equally horrible – but nevertheless they are classes rather than one class, which has rather sinister connotations. At any rate, he had *heard* about the working classes, but he had never seen any. You don't, you know, in Eton; you never see any. What he had seen was tramps and beggars and winos in the streets. He could not help but observe them, just walking around in the streets in the late 1920s anywhere in the country, but particularly in London. And he thought, of course, that these were the working classes that he had heard about. Because he was a do-er and an actor; because he wanted to go and do things rather than just think about them, he thought "well, I'd better just go and find out what it's all about".

So he did, in a quite extraordinary way, become a tramp, a wino, someone who hung around the streets with no money at all. He lived in doss-houses and worked in restaurants both in London and in Paris. He wrote a very fine book called *Down and Out in Paris and London* which describes all these

Unemployed in 1939 Wigan: Photograph Kurt Hutton

terrible things that are happening literally in the gutter of society - but without really coming into contact with the people that he had heard about, and in a sense *wanted* to contact in some way, these working classes that he had read about at Eton.

Wigan Pier

He did not really come into contact with them until he was commissioned to write a book about the condition of the English working class. That was the original title. Of course, it has a much more famous pedigree! But he was to write a book about the condition of the English working class in the north. So, he travelled, for the first time, north, and went to live among working-class people and saw how they lived and described how they lived and worked in his first really great book, which is *The Road to Wigan Pier*.

His descriptions are still very valuable to us. He met the miners, and described in the most graphic detail what it was like to be a miner, a thing that shocked him to his roots. The description is good enough, but the conclusion is even better – something that is as useful today as anything you would want to read about the miners anywhere, at any place.

"More than anyone else, perhaps, the miner can stand as the type of the manual worker, not only because his work is so exaggeratedly awful, but also because it is so vitally necessary and yet so remote from our experience, so invisible, as it were, that we are capable of forgetting it as we forget the blood in our veins. In a way, it is even humiliating to watch coal-miners working. It raises in you a momentary doubt about your own status as an "intellectual" and a superior person generally. For it is brought home to you, at least while you are watching, that it is only because miners sweat their guts out that superior persons can remain superior. You and I and the editor of the *Times Literary Supplement*, [4] and the Archbishop of Canterbury and Comrade X, author of *Marxism for Infants* – all of us really owe the comparative decency of our lives to poor drudges underground, blackened to the eyes, with their throats full of coal dust, driving their shovels forward with arms and belly muscles of steel."

That is how he described the miners in *The Road to Wigan Pier*, and the description is just as relevant to us, just as crucial to us in all the propaganda that we make about miners today. But there is a strange gap in the book. It is almost as if there is a hiatus, as if you have come to a river and do not cross it because the bridge is not there. You get a real feeling of the conditions that workers lived in, the dreadful conditions in their houses, the dreadful conditions in the places that they worked. You get a real feeling of the warmth and decency of working-class people, as opposed to the people among whom Orwell had moved up to that time. But you get no feeling at all, throughout the whole book, of their *strength* and their power; no feeling of the collective action which can change these conditions.

People say, "well there were no strikes in the 1930s; it was a bad time. There was nothing happening." It is not true.

The curious thing is that just as Orwell was preparing to write his book in which the miners play such a prominent part, as he was describing what miners do, and seeing how important it was, the things that they were doing, there was a strike starting – one of the biggest strikes of the 1930s, at Harworth Colliery in Nottingham. A strike to do with the formation of a break-away union from the Federation of Mineworkers. It was a very, very long, brutal and tough strike. And the first two or three months of it took place while Orwell was writing his book. Yet there is not a single reference to that strike, or to any other strike. There is nothing on the way in which trade unions work, nor indeed to how the relationship between the trade union leadership and the rank and file worker operates. All of these things were out of his ken, something that he either had not discovered, or refused to discover. He showed no interest in them at all.

There is a relevance in this gap in Orwell's writing. It is not just that we can say "Aha! Missed out on the struggle. Missed out on the collective spirit. Wrong again, George. Bad luck. Pity you did not meet one of us at the time." It is more important than that. He discusses the whole politics of the 1930s, and you see the importance of the gap when it comes to his political analysis. Of course, he is interested in getting socialism and he says this in the last part of his book. The first bit is descriptive; the second bit is what we can do. Part of it is very relevant today – in fact it is an absolutely accurate account of exactly what is going on:

"A generation ago every intelligent person was in some sense a revolutionary; nowadays it would be nearer the mark to say that every intelligent person is a reactionary."

He says a generation ago, he means when he was a young man in the early 1920s, it seemed to him that every intelligent person, by which of course he means every middle-class person, because he did not know anybody else, was a revolutionary.

Who's important? "Lenin" at Eton. It did not

make any difference to their lives, but they thought they were interested in it, they had some concern about what was going on in Russia.

In the 1930s, exactly the opposite.

Now that is very relevant to us today, is it not? I remember in the early 1970s we went around to rich middle-class people trying to get money for the International Socialists. We would go to see all kinds of people: the names would be quite extraordinary to repeat them now. They were fantastically interested in what was going on in the revolution. They would stop their Volvo cars and jump out and say, "Tell us about the revolution". "What is this about the revolution?". I remember, just after I had gone to work at *Socialist Worker*, a cheque for £17,000 arriving with a letter from someone in the north saying, "Here, comrade, is the inheritance I have received today. I renounce my inheritance and declare my solidarity with International Socialism".

This was widespread. The middle class, like a weathercock, blowing with the wind, at that time as in the 1920s were fantastically interested. 1930s, they were not. 1980s, they are not. They hate it, hate us, all of these people who gave us money. "Give it back. Where's my inheritance?"

All over society, all over the universities, there's this tremendous drift to the right. The middle class is *not* with us today, not even a sprinkling of them moving in our direction. That is something that has stopped.

The change that he noticed in the 1920s and 1930s is the same as it is now. And there is a conundrum, a riddle about it – which he kept putting to himself, that he could not really understand. It was this question:

"What I am concerned with is the fact that socialism is losing ground exactly where it ought to be gaining it. With so much in its favour, for every empty belly is an argument for socialism – the idea of socialism is less widely accepted than it was ten years ago. The average thinking person nowadays is not merely not a socialist, he is actively hostile to socialism."

Again, when he says "the average thinking person" he still means those people in polite society in London, but nevertheless there is a truth in it, isn't there?

For us today there is also this conundrum, this riddle. There is capitalist society, in the 1930s and in the 1980s, utterly bankrupt. There are people stacked up with starvation. All the time more and more starvation. All the time more and more unemployment. The system completely unable to cope with its problems and its crises. The argument for a different kind of system, for planning the economy, for meeting production with need, all these elementary arguments quite obviously stronger when reflected against the objective facts of the society, than they were ten years ago – than they were either in the 1970s or comparing the 1930s to the 1920s.

These are circumstances in which you would expect, and Orwell expects, the movement for socialism to grow – for more and more people to become socialists because the argument was so plain. And yet the opposite was happening.

Orwell said to himself: now, let's address ourselves to that problem, as an intellectual. Let's look at the problem and see, why, with such powerful arguments, less and less people are accepting it. The conclusion, the reason is that they are confused by socialists. They don't like socialists, that's the problem. And in *The Road to Wigan Pier*, he makes the famous attack on socialists.

Socialists are "people who drink carrot juice", "people who have large bottoms, and walk around in shorts" are all kinds of weirdos and loons and so on. This is often cited as being quite funny, because it does describe people that we know, and we think this is very good. Sometimes you see it cited as dealing with middle-class socialists – "wasn't he funny about middle-class socialists, wasn't it a joke the things he said about carrot juice and fat bottoms, and didn't it accurately describe the ILP[5] at the time?"

I think it is a fundamental mistake to believe that the downturn – the reason why people had abandoned the ideas of socialism - was because the socialists were so distasteful. If only we could drink good beer instead of carrot juice, and thin down our bums, and perhaps start talking in a slightly better way, then that would change. Socialists would appeal more strongly to the people they were trying to get to.

It obviously was *not* the problem. This comes from the same book:

"There are, I believe, countless people who, without being aware of it, are in sympathy with the essential ends of socialism, and who could be won over almost without a struggle if only one could find the word that would move them."

Now that reminds me very much of certain orthodox Trotskyists. They developed a theory of socialism that was founded on what I call the "fruit machine" notion. The fruit machine notion is based on the idea that you pull a lever – that's what you do, I think, with fruit machines – you pull a lever and apples come up in the right order. And if they come up in the right order, the cash comes out. Now their notion about the working class not being socialist – because they hadn't got a programme - and if only we could fit in 300 nationalised companies, troops out of Ireland, a few other things, in the slot machine and pull the lever, somehow or other the revolution would come.

And that is what it is, this thing he says: "If only one could find the *word* that would move them". If only one could find the right word we'll be able to galvanise the masses. It very much reminds me of that kind of thinking.

And again it reverts back to the gap in that book, the hiatus that exists in that book, because the real reasons for the downturn in the 1930s were very, very similar to the real reasons for the downturn in the 1980s. The real underlying causes are roughly the same. 1920s: the reason for it could be summed up in two words really: General Strike. 1926: catastrophe, slaughter for the miners, breakdown of the trade union movement, general lack of confidence going on and on and leading to mass unemployment in the early 1930s. Those are the things that cause people to lose their confidence.

GEORGE ORWELL & **1984**

In other words, this lack of knowledge of the workers' strength leads him away from any understanding of what it was that created the conditions for socialism, or for thinking about socialism. What people *do* in the working class, how they act, how they direct themselves, how they organise, have to do with how they think, and when they don't feel confident enough to do things, or they *don't* do things, and they don't use their power and strength, their confidences goes, it vanishes, and as their confidence vanishes so their belief and confidence in socialist ideas also vanishes. The two things go on at the same time. In other words that connection between the movement of the class, these shimmering ups and downs, as the class moves up and down, that connection was lost to him when he talked about the miners, lost to him when he talked about the other workers and therefore lost to him when it came to a solution. What to do about it had to do with socialists getting into "longs" and not shorts, wearing sports jackets, ties and looking ordinary and decent and not looking frumpy and cranky – and that was the way in which you could change it, as though that would really have made any great difference to the downturn of the 1930s.

He refused to accept this connection between the confidence of the working class and their strength – and that is the great gap that exists in *The Road to Wigan Pier* and leads him into the sort of wildernesses that exist at the end of that book.

And if that had been the end of it, in other words if Orwell was a theoretician, someone who just *thought* things, really he would have stewed in that book. We would not be discussing him today. He would not be relevant. There would not be articles in *International Socialism* journal and *Socialist Review* about him.

But he wasn't just a theoretician, that's the point about him. He was a do-er. He did things. And when he watched what was happening in the world he saw what was going on in Spain; he saw the fascist attack on Spain and the revolution that took place in whole areas of Spain as a result of that, and his immediate instinct was to do something about it.

Barcelona

Here is a scene in a newspaper in London – rather nice, middle-class, following the policies of "social credit" and the like – and here is the editor sitting behind his desk and this great shambling figure comes in with a rucksack saying "I'm sorry, can't write my column this week. I'm off to Spain"

"Why are you off to Spain?"

"This fascism thing, it's got to be stopped."

And he's going to stop it.

Now Orwell arrived in revolutionary Barcelona in December 1936, and he spent six months in Spain fighting fascists. And he chronicled those six months in what is, beyond any question at all, the greatest book he wrote, his greatest writing: *Homage to Catalonia*.

If there is any SWP member who has not read *Homage to Catalonia* then that is something about which they should be deeply ashamed. If there is any member who has read *1984* and *Animal Farm*,

Barcelona 1936

but has not read *Homage to Catalonia*, then that is a catastrophe.

Homage to Catalonia is a truly magnificent book. Paul O'Flinn in *International Socialism* journal confesses that he was pulled out of Oxfam Quakerism by reading the first three pages of *Homage to Catalonia*. I remember twenty-four years ago, as the President of the Oxford University Liberal Club, picking up this book, and just on the third page reading this. It had exactly the same effect on me as it had on Paul O'Flinn, as I think it has on many others:

> "It was the first time that I had ever been in a town where the working class was in the saddle. Practically every building of any size had been seized by the workers, and was draped with red flags or with the red-and-black flag of the anarchists. Every wall was scrawled with the hammer and sickle and with the initials of revolutionary parties. Almost every church had been gutted, and its images burnt. Churches, here and there, were being systematically demolished by gangs of workmen. Every shop and café had an inscription saying that it had been collectivised. Even the boot-blacks had been collectivised and their boxes painted red and black. Waiters and shop-keepers looked you in the face and treated you as an equal. Servile and even ceremonial forms of speech had temporarily disappeared. Nobody said "Senor" or "Don" or even "Usted". Everyone called everyone else "Comrade" and "Thou", and said "Salud" instead of "Buenos dias". Tipping was forbidden by law. Almost my first experience was receiving a lecture from a hotel manager for trying to tip a lift-boy. There were no private motor cars, they had all been commandeered, and all the trams and taxis and much of the other transport were painted red and black. The revolutionary posters were everywhere, flaming from the walls in clean reds and blues that

made the few remaining advertisements look like daubs of mud. Down in the Ramblas, the wide central artery of the town, where crowds of people streamed constantly to and fro, the loudspeakers were bellowing revolutionary songs all day and far into the night. And it was the aspect of the crowds that was the queerest thing of all. In outward appearance it was a town in which the wealthy classes had practically ceased to exist. Except for a small number of women and foreigners, there were no "well-dressed" people at all. Practically everyone wore rough working-class clothes or blue overalls, or some variant of the militia uniform. All this was queer and moving. There was much in it that I did not understand; in some ways I did not even like it. But I recognised it immediately as a state of affairs worth fighting for."

That image, and that picture, goes on and on in the book. I will just give one more passage, when Orwell goes to the Front itself. I think this is probably some of the finest revolutionary writing in our literature, if not *the* finest. It describes his experience on the Front, fighting the fascists with the militia:

"However much one cursed at the time, one realised afterwards that one had been in contact with something strange and valuable. One had been in a community where hope was more normal than apathy or cynicism, where the word "comrade" stood for comradeship, and not, as in most countries, for humbug. One had breathed the air of equality. I'm well aware that it is now the fashion to deny that socialism has anything to do with equality. In every country

in the world a huge tribe of party-hacks and
sleek little professors are busy "proving" that
socialism means no more than a planned state
capitalism with the grab-motive left intact.
But fortunately there also exists a vision of
socialism quite different from this. The thing
that attracts ordinary men to socialism, and
makes them willing to risk their skins for it, the
"mystique" of socialism, *is* the idea of equality;
to the vast majority of people socialism means a
classless society, or it means nothing at all. And
it was here that those few months in the militia
were valuable to me. For the Spanish militias,
while they lasted, were a sort of microcosm of
a classless society. In that community where
no one was on the make, where there was a
shortage of everything but no privilege and no
boot-licking, one got, perhaps, a crude forecast
of what the opening stages of socialism might be
like. And, after all, instead of disillusioning me, it
deeply attracted me. The effect was to make my
desire to see socialism established much more
actual than it had been before."

It filled the gap that was in *The Road to Wigan Pier*. It filled it not just metaphorically, but it filled it literally. He wrote this:

"The way in which the working class in the
democratic countries could really have helped
her Spanish comrades was by industrial action -
strikes and boycotts."

I have read, I think, most of Orwell and I don't remember a single other reference in any of his work to strikes or boycotts, particularly to strikes.

GEORGE ORWELL & **1984**

That is the reference. And that is the reference that comes at a time when he sees the working class, not only in action, but in control. And when he sees them in action and control, the cobwebs of the kind of socialism that he described and talked about in *The Road to Wigan Pier* are wiped clean.

Not only are the cobwebs wiped clean, but the *politics* of the situation become stark and clear. He writes about the Spanish situation, thinking that he had gone – don't forget – to fight a war against fascism for republicanism, he writes as he comes back from Spain itself:

> "The real struggle is between revolution and counter-revolution, between the workers who are vainly trying to hold on to a little of what they won in 1936 and the Liberal-Communist bloc, who are so successfully taking it away from them. It is unfortunate that so few people in England have yet caught up with the fact that Communism is now a counter-revolutionary force, that Communists everywhere are in alliance with bourgeois reformism and using the whole of their powerful machinery to crush or discredit any party that shows signs of revolutionary tendencies."

Now that is in 1937. Long before most people were aware of these facts. And the reason he was aware of it was that he had **seen** the successful revolution. Every day of those six months that he spent in Spain he could see the effect of the counter-revolution on what he had seen. What mattered to him was that the wonderful image of Barcelona, which he saw when he arrived, was gradually changed in front of his eyes. When he went back there on leave it was a different city. There were wealthy people on the streets. The expressions of deference had begun to grow back into people's mouths, they were beginning to bow and scrape. The thing was changing, and it was changing by the deliberate act of a liberal government backed up by the Communists.

Seeing it shook him to his roots. That is part of the IS tradition, if anything is.

When he had gone to Spain he was quite prepared to go and fight in the International Brigade alongside other Communists. He knew that the Communists had supplied far more fighters in the International Brigade than any other section. But when he got there he saw how the Communists were in league with the Liberal alliance, with the Liberal government in order to destroy the revolution, to take it away.

And that was the problem. It was not just fascism that was the problem - the whole business of fighting fascism – and he describes it in that book – the discipline that exists in the line, the revolutionary discipline which gets people to do things because they believe in it, that never orders anybody to do anything, that does not have hierarchies or badges of rank, but expects volunteers to come forward, as they *did* consistently and constantly during the six months that he was there and for the most daring and horrible things, expects them to come forward because they are part of a movement. Under *those* circumstances fascism could be beaten. With sleek, well-equipped armies, with weapons from Russia and with all the ranks and insignia of ranks that existed in "proper" armies, fascism could not be beaten.

These things were *crucial*. The problem was the revolution against the counter-revolution – the revolution had to be defended. And when the events took place in May he was with the POUM[6], he was desperately trying to keep away the counter-revolution, and of course failed to do it.

Now the thing that struck him was not really so much that the Liberal government was against revolution. He might have predicted that. But the thing that struck him, and struck him all the way through the rest of his life, almost every day of it, was this business of the Communist Party allying themselves with the counter-revolution.

"It is not a nice thing to see a Spanish boy of fifteen carried down the line on a stretcher with a dazed, white face looking out from under the blankets, and to think of the sleek persons in London and Paris who are writing pamphlets to prove that this boy is a fascist in disguise."

They were liars and cheats and they were defaming the revolutionaries all down the line, and he *saw* that they were defaming them. The most powerful chapter in the book is the one where he deals with the arguments, in an almost Etonian fashion.

But he deals with it factually, pointing out not only were they not in the fascist pay, but they were the most *bitter* opponents – and the most *effective* opponents of the fascists. And the counter-revolution, although he did not predict it at the time, effectively destroyed the republican side in the Spanish Civil War and established fascism there for forty or fifty years.

From then the fury of the double-dealing hypocrisy of the Communists moved him all of his life. It is impossible really to appreciate all the things that Orwell later wrote unless you understand that fact. How deeply he was enraged by the role of the Communists in Spain. The only thing that I have seen similar to it, similar to the *passion* that comes out of him about it, is the book by Victor Serge, *The Case of Comrade Tulayev,* the fifth chapter of which deals with revolutionary Spain and the role of the Communists in it. Serge and Orwell had a great deal in common with each other, and with us, and they both detected with passion and with their tremendous descriptive powers just what it meant when you found that the people who are meant to be at the very centre of the revolution were the people who were destroying it. And how all the people all over the world calling themselves Communists and believing themselves to be part of a revolutionary process, were in fact part of a machine that was destroying that revolutionary process.

Back from Spain

When Orwell came back from Spain, he joined the ILP. Now the ILP hardly existed. It was a rump. He joined it just because he thought he should join something and he didn't know anything else to join. He does not seem to have had any *part* of any party, or even of that party, during any part of his life. But his politics were very much to the left of the ILP. All the way through the late 1930s he continued his tirades against what he called "the anti-fascist racket". He wrote to Herbert Read in January 1939:

"I believe it is vitally necessary for those of us who intend to oppose the coming war to start organising for illegal anti-war activities."

And his vision of society then was of imperialist war, people fighting each other, all with interests which no socialist could defend, a gradual move to dictatorship in all the different countries, and the few socialists that opposed it going underground, illegally agitating – perhaps actually fighting – against their government in the interests of the workers all over the world.

That was his position in 1938 and 1939. But of course as soon as war broke out he did change it. Not only him, by the way.....almost everyone on the left went over to some kind of defencism, to some kind of support for the war. If you were in the Communist Party you were absolutely mad for the war, hysterical for the war, wonderful war that was being fought. As you moved further left so the enthusiasm for the war effort actually declined. Now Orwell went over to the war. He wrote a series of articles brought out in one of those Collected Works, *My Country Right or Left*. And that was his position, and he was quite frank about it, appalling though it may sound now.

But I think it is important to remember that all the way through the war he never really lost that vision of Barcelona. He never lost his belief in the working class, and he never really collapsed into chauvinism or jingoism or any of the rubbish that was coming from the Communist Party and other sections of the left.

"That rifle hanging on the wall of the working-class flat or labourer's cottage is the symbol of democracy" he wrote in the middle of the war. "It is our job to see that it stays there."

Now that is *not* the writing of some bourgeois reformist. That rifle – you keep it. I am in the Home Guard and have got to get as many rifles into the houses of working-class people as I possibly can.

Here he's writing in *Tribune* [7]. Amazing: *Tribune*!

"It is only by revolution that the English can be set free."

That is in *Tribune*. That is the only time that sentiment has ever appeared in *Tribune*.

And as he saw the Communists snuggle up closer to the Tories....It's difficult to imagine it in a way, looking back on it now, but you have to see it as it was then. The Communists and the Tories snuggling up to one another. The Communist Party never wanted Labour to fight the 1945 election; they wanted the coalition to continue; they were worried that Labour would not win it – or they were worried that Labour *would* win it. I am not sure what they were worried about. They did not want an election and they put out pamphlets saying in some cases to vote for progressive Tories – like Churchill and Eden, and so on. [8]

As he saw this alliance continue towards the end of the war, he got more and more furious at it. In particular he singled out Poland. He said, look at the rape of Poland! You go to Tehran, or you go to Yalta, or you go to Potsdam – Stalin, Churchill, Roosevelt, people of that kind dividing up the world.

Yalta Conference 1945, Churchill, Roosevelt, and Stalin divide up the world.

Where is your support for Poland? You were against the fascist invasion of Poland; you were against the annexation then; why are you not against them now?

He railed against them, banged against them, constantly exposed the double standard which they represented. And at the same time – and this is important – he never lost his position. He never allowed himself to slide to the right. This is *very* important when people say "those sales figures for *1984* you gave me at the beginning, they represent the American government, the British government, international capitalism sanctioning this book, using it in their university examinations and the like, and promoting it. Didn't he just slide over, as another cold warrior?"

Answer. No he did not.

We are talking of different times. The Duchess of Atholl, who was a Tory, wrote and asked him to speak at an anti-Russian meeting. He replied, in November 1945:

> "I cannot associate myself with an essentially Conservative body which claims to defend democracy in Europe but has nothing to say about British imperialism. It seems to me that one can only denounce the crimes now being committed in Poland, Yugoslavia, etc, if one is equally insistent on ending Britain's unwanted rule in India. I belong to the Left and must work inside it."

And he went on and on against race prejudice..... against the Germans. He was absolutely opposed to the anti-German prejudice. There is a very curious little correspondence in his letters, where somebody writes in to *Tribune* saying: "Well I, like you, want the Hun to be beaten" and he wrote this:

> "Now, it seems to me that you do less harm by dropping bombs on people than by calling them "Huns"...War damages the fabric of civilisation not by the destruction it causes...but by stimulating hatred."

Now that is obviously rubbish. It is perverse, is it not. It is perverse to say that you do more damage to someone by calling him or her a Hun than by dropping a bomb. I mean that is wrong, clearly wrong. But you see what he is saying, "I'd rather drop the bombs on them than have any racial divisions come out here, that poison, the future wars, reparations and the like." He maintained that feeling, that the Germans were people just like

GEORGE ORWELL & **1984**

anyone else, the German workers were workers like anyone else. He maintained it.

In spite of his position on the war he did not slide right over into what we now know – but which wasn't then, I emphasise that, which was not then – cold war rhetoric. But his preoccupation remained the same and we are lucky, in a way, that it did. The preoccupation remained: Russia. What the Russian government did in Spain. What the Russian government did all through those periods of the purges. How the Russian government dealt with opposition. How the Russian government dealt with working-class organisation.

It was his preoccupation, and almost no-one else's at this time. The destruction of the Soviet myth is essential if we want the revival of the socialist movement. When I started out, the thing that mattered most of all, the question that kept coming back on socialism all the time was: "What about Russia?" Still happens. "Go back to Russia." Not so much now – even a blind idiot can see there is no connection between Russia and socialism now. But still they do say it and still it is an argument even today.

Those Two Books

The fact that he was identifying it in 1945 is absolutely crucial to understanding Orwell. It was that aim, that inspiration that led him to write these last two books which are by far his most famous, these two satires on the Russian model, *Animal Farm* published in 1945 and *1984*, which was published in 1949, although written in 1947 and 1948.

They *are* on the Russian model. I do not go along with the people who say "Oh, you know, it was really *all* bureaucracy that he was against." You only have to read the books again. I read them again, and there is no question.

No question at all about *Animal Farm*, obviously. In my belief, no question at all that *1984* is also on the Russian model. Even the names are similar. Goldstein for Bronstein. There is no question that Goldstein the figure in *1984* – internationalism coming out again, by the way; his hatred of anti-Semitism: his hero is a Jew – but the names Goldstein and Bronstein are too similar not to believe that Goldstein *is* a Trotsky figure in *1984* [9]. It is on the Russian model.

And it is important to say it again: that these books are not written at the time of the Cold War, as we now know it. Maybe he should have foreseen it. But that time, 1945, 1946, 1947, it was not a Cold War time. This was a time when Stalinist Russia, conservative Britain – or later Labour Britain – and the conservatives in the United States of America were coming together, it seemed to him – and *rightly* seemed to him as we now know it, although precious few people knew it then – to suppress the rising aspirations of the working-class people where he placed his allegiance.

It is also important that the working class *is still there* in those books. I mean these are pessimistic books, I agree. Paul O'Flinn has a terrific attack on *1984* – but the working class is still in this book, this 750,000 copies going around. It is still there. It's passive; it's back to the passivity of *The Road to Wigan Pier* and it is rather dull and obscure, and in some ways insulted, but they are there all right and they are not just there mentioned in passing, they are there as the only hope of civilisation.

"If there is hope," wrote Winston, "it lies in the proles. If there was hope it *must* lie in the proles, because only there in those swarming disregarded masses could the force to destroy the Party be generated." (Party, of course, representing bureaucracy and power.)

The same riddle and conundrum which had bothered Orwell in *The Road to Wigan Pier* comes out again. Remember Winston Smith writing in the corners away from the television screens, trying to work it out for himself. There are all the elements of this attempting to come to grips with the problems. How can we change it? Writing it down there, writing the sentence:

"Until they become conscious they will never rebel, and until after they have rebelled they cannot become conscious."

Say it again. Until they become conscious, they will never rebel. But until after they have rebelled, they cannot become conscious. An awful Catch-22 but one which leaves out the fact that the rebellion is going on all the time in the struggle. It is the same gap that existed there in *The Road to Wigan Pier*. He had seen a successful revolution, or the ending of a successful revolution, but he had never seen or fitted into the struggle and therefore he is forced to argue: How do we get the consciousness? How do we get the proles off their backs? How do we get them moving? How do we turn their strength into consciousness and mingle the consciousness with the strength?

That's the problem, and that Catch-22 situation seemed to exist. Here is the extract that I think is the central piece in *1984*. Just before Winston and Julia are taken away by the police and smashed to pieces in the torture chambers, just before that happens, the very climax of the book in my belief:

> "The future belonged to the proles, " this is Smith thinking. "And could he be sure that when their time came the world they constructed would not be just as alien to him, Winston Smith, as the world of the Party. Yes, because at the least it would be a world of sanity. Where there is equality there can be sanity. Sooner or later it would happen, strength would change into consciousness. The proles were immortal, you could not doubt it when you looked at that valiant figure in the yard."

And then he goes on to say how it may take a thousand years to happen but it will happen in the end, that they will come into it.

Now a thousand years is too long for me. I am not going to wait a thousand years. I think the future lies with the proles, but I am not going to wait a thousand years and I am not going to put up with any Central Committee document which comes around, perspectives for the next thousand years. *1984 is* very pessimistic. It does not have the strength. It has lost the strength of Barcelona and the weakness and passivity of Wigan Pier is back.

I will just make this point finally in Orwell's defence, and some say in defence of the book. If Orwell was just a left social democrat like Bernard Crick says in his, on the whole, very good 1980 biography,[10] if he was a left Tribunite, somebody who wanted the left of the Labour Party to triumph, and if – as is certainly the case – *1984* is an extremely pessimistic book, why did he write it then? You see, if you were a social democrat in the immediate post-war years – if you were someone who thought that the election of Labour governments is what matters, and even if you were someone who thought that the election of Labour governments would lead to things happening – then the years in which he wrote these two books were the summer, the high peak. If you were a Stalinist in 1947, things were good. Things were looking up; Stalinism was rampant throughout Eastern Europe; they had imposed it by bayonet throughout six countries in Eastern Europe; they seemed to be a very, very powerful force with fantastic influence.

But the point is: if you were a Labour person, a left Labour person, a supporter of Aneurin Bevan, then this was a great time, this was terrific. Everything would seem to be bursting with activity and life. All those nationalisation acts, 1946, 1947, Industrial Injury Acts, National Health Service on the agenda, Labour government with a majority of 145, Aneurin Bevan in the Cabinet and sponsoring all those articles in *Tribune* in the late 1940s. It was great. It was wonderful. It was a great time to be a social democrat.

The most obscure question of all is therefore,

why he should write such an utterly gloomy book about the oncoming totalitarianism if he was a left Tribunite? If he was a Tribunite, he should have been dancing in the streets: Great, we've got it! We're there!

The reason he wrote it was not just, in my belief, that he hated the Russians – which he did. He hated the Communist Party, and this hatred had obscured his belief in working-class power. I think that he also sensed, long before most other people did, for most other people weren't feeling it – he sensed in a vague sort of way that this Labour government, this Labourism, this great wet blanket was coming and covering the whole of the working-class movement. Keep down, shut up, wait till elections, then you can come up for a little bit, but for Chrissake get back in your holes again. Don't do anything after the election, keep quiet, don't think, don't agitate, don't talk, for Chrissake don't go on strike – if you go on strike we will smash you to pieces. All these things happened in the 1945-51 government. Capitalism was re-asserted after fantastic aspirations had grown up as a result of the war.

I think he sensed it. I think he thought that this Labour government is not a bulwark against oncoming totalitarianism. He said: I am not writing against Russia for capitalism; I am against capitalism. He put out two press releases immediately after *1984* came out, when it started to be praised in America and all the McCarthyites – or the McCarthyites in embryo – started to get hold of the thing and praise it and say: This is the book for us. The fact that they could do it is a criticism of

Orwell, and the book is reactionary and pessimistic in many ways, but the reasons why he wrote it, I believe, have to do with the fact that the things he *really* believed in, which were the movements from below, the activity, the rank and file working-class people, were being suppressed by the Labour government as they were by the rising Stalinism in Russia. And I think in a sense that is a question that the Crick's of this world never really come to answer.

One to Him, One from Him

I just want to go back finally to where I started, and ask the question: What is it that he can give us, and what is it that we can give him, this great, shambling old Etonian, this "Trotskyist with big feet" as H.G. Wells called him?

Well, one thing he did not have was something like we have got in the SWP. He had not got the collective, and the feeling of the collective, and the confidence that the collective gives you. He was a socialist, but he was not the sort of socialist who realised that you have to *pool* your abilities and resources if your abilities and resources are going to be of any use whatever. He did not realise that it is in collaboration and co-operation with others, connected with that other thing that he missed almost all his life, except the brief months in Barcelona, connected with the *movement* of the working class, the power that they have to change society, the collective of socialists connected up with that movement – he did not have that. I think that if he'd had that he would have been

Trotsky in Mexico 1940.

a better writer.

But I also think that it is quite pointless saying "Oh perhaps he would have been alright if he'd met the right person." I notice John Deason says in his article: "Oh if he'd only met Reg Groves when he was working in the bookshop, because Reg Groves went to work there." Well actually he did meet Reg Groves, and it didn't make any difference.[11]

Meeting Reg Groves does not change your life. It is silly to say: "Oh poor old Orwell never came into contact with any decent Trotskyists, and he blundered around". People do say that. I think that is silly. I think he was hostile, to be honest. There is plenty of evidence that he was hostile to quite a lot of Trotskyism. I have got an example here:

> "Sometimes, when I listen to these people talking, and still more when I read their books, I get the impression that, to them, the whole socialist movement is no more than a kind of exciting heresy hunt – a leaping to and fro of frenzied witch-doctors to the beat of tom-toms and the tune of Fee-fie-fo-fum I smell the blood of a right-wing deviationist."

I think he had come in contact with us all right![12]

We have got that to give him, but the other question I ask is what has he got to give us? I think that is also a very important question.

We have a collective. I think sometimes people think that the collective is just a lot of people speaking with one voice. Now, it is a lot of people speaking with one voice, but it is very important that the one voice is divided into hundreds, if not thousands of different accents and different languages. I think people sometimes think that being in a collective enables them to surrender their duty to think each subject through. And I think the great advantage of Orwell is that he thought everything through for himself.

That is the first great advantage. But you can never convince anyone in argument – and we have no other way of convincing them – unless *they* are convinced that *you* believe it. Not that you are saying it because you heard someone else saying it, or that you are taking it by rote.

The collective is many different people and that cannot mean sameness. If socialism was the same as sameness then there would be no point in fighting for it. If a socialist party was the same as sameness there would be no point in fighting for it. The point is that we speak with one voice, but every one of us is different. And every one of us arrives at the conclusion for different reasons, and in different ways. And the importance of thinking it through, and arguing it through for yourself is something which I think comes very clearly out of what Orwell has to say.

Trotsky's assassin, who had come along with an article written in terms of which he thought Trotsky would approve, had actually written it in dull, sectarian language. Although it was correct from start to finish, Trotsky could immediately see the problem and the last thing he said before the axe went into his head was "Write plainly, comrade." Those were his last words. You have got to learn to write plainly.

I think this business of writing simply, and not talking in absurd, sectarian jargon, not the name-calling, the awful culture-hunting which goes on with people who think that because they are in the collective they can be aggressive and unpleasant about it without the independent thought coming out. All those things I think are terribly important coming out of Orwell. It is a great legacy which we have got from him, this sparkling clarity of his language.

I said earlier that language was not *the* important thing in changing working-class consciousness. Of course it is not *the* important thing, but it is definitely *an* important thing. Prose should be like a window-pane. You should be able to see through language, to its meaning. If you cannot see through language to its meaning it is absolutely appalling. It has a reverse effect. The more you talk in language which does not mean anything, the more people will not believe you, because they believe you are getting it from someone else.

Here is Orwell on Professor Harold Laski:

"As a whole, our system was a compromise between democracy in the political realm - itself a very recent development in our history - and an economic power oligarchically organised which was in its turn related to a certain aristocratic vestigia still able to influence profoundly the habits of our society."

He continues:

"This sentence, incidentally, comes from a reprinted lecture; so one must assume that Professor Laski actually stood up on a platform and spouted it forth, parenthesis and all. It is clear that people capable of speaking or writing in such a way have simply forgotten what everyday language is like. But this is nothing to some of the other passages I could dig out of Professor Laski's writing, or better still, from Communist literature, or best of all, from Trotskyist pamphlets. Indeed, from reading the left-wing press, you get the impression that the louder people yap about the proletariat, the more they despise its language."

I think we *do* have a lesson there. I think if we can learn our *own* language, to speak our own language more, we can cut away all the time from things that have been passed down to us, learn to think things through and talk ourselves **as** part of the collective. Then we can start to blend a real language, a real communicating spirit with the people outside, with the power that we already have, the power to change *and* the power to communicate.

We have got one to contribute to him. He has got one to contribute to us. And let us hope that together we go forward to hear *nothing... nothing* we cannot aim at and *nothing* we cannot achieve.

Notes

1. "George Orwell: International Socialist? 1. The Development of Orwell's Socialism" in *International Socialism* (First Series) Number 37 June-July 1969 pp. 28-34. *https:// www.marxists.org/archive/sedgwick/1969/xx/orwell.htm*
2. "1984 was his worst book" by John Deason in *Socialist Review* Issue 61 January 1984 pp. 28-30.
3. "Re-Reading Nineteen Eighty-Four in 1984" by Paul O'Flinn in *International Socialism Journal* (Second Series) Number 23, Spring 1984 pp. 76-98. *https://www.marxists. org/history/etol/writers/oflinn/1984/xx/1984.html*
4. The Bookmarks Publications transcript of Paul's talk shows that he omitted to read the words "and the Nancy poets" that are written by Orwell in his published work.
5. The Independent Labour Party was established in 1893. It disaffiliated from the Labour Party in 1932 with politics consistently to the left of Labour. It was active in the Republican

cause during the Spanish Civil War.

6. The Partido Obrero de Unificación Marxista (The Workers' Party of Marxist Unification), generally known as POUM, was a revolutionary organisation founded in Spain in 1935. Its leader Andres Nin, a Trotskyist, but one who broke with Trotsky over questions of tactics, was murdered by the Stalinists in June 1937. Orwell served with the POUM militia in Spain.

7. *Tribune* was a democratic socialist magazine founded in 1937. It supported the Labour Party from the left. Orwell joined *Tribune* as its Literary Editor in 1943.

8. Paul is not describing the CPGB's *final* 1945 General Election position. For a useful precis of their *initial* position versus their *later* position see pp. 32-33 in *"Workers against the Monolith: The Communist Parties Since 1943"* by Ian Birchall, 1974 Pluto Press, London, 256pp. The CPGB Executive Committee explained away their initial profound political error in a *"Political Letter to Members"* dated 28th August 1945 as follows: "It is now clear, in the light of the election results and the political development that has taken place, that the proposal (put forward after the Crimea Conference) to form a National Government, including Tories, after the election was not politically justified, and reflected (1) under-estimation of the degree of the Left swing, which made possible the return of an overwhelming Labour majority; (2) over-estimation of the degree of differentiation in the Tory Party and of the possibility and necessity of securing the co-operation of the pro-Crimea elements against the Fifth Column elements who opposed Crimea." [NB: Crimea Conference is another name for the Yalta Conference of February 1945].

9. Leon Trotsky's real name was Lev Davidovich Bronstein.

10. *"George Orwell: A Life"* by Bernard Crick. 1980. Secker & Warburg, Ltd., London, 656pp.

11. Reg Groves was a member of the Balham Group and one of the earliest British Trotskyists.

12. The quote is from *The Road to Wigan Pier*. Orwell did know the Trotskyists. His pamphlet collection contained numerous Trotskyist titles. In 1946 he was approached by the Revolutionary Communist Party and asked to sign a public statement titled Nuremburg and the Moscow Trials. The statement called for the slander against Trotskyists during the Moscow Trials to be investigated and that a representative of Natalia Trotsky attend the Nuremberg Trials. Not only did Orwell sign the statement but he followed up with a second letter to the secretary of the RCP suggesting further names to be approached. The correspondence appears in Volume 18 of *The Complete Works of George Orwell*.